Teaching Strategies & Techniques
for Adjunct Faculty
SECOND EDITION

Donald Greive, Ed.D.

INFO-TEC, Inc. • Cleveland, Ohio

Order Information:

INFO-TEC, Inc.
P.O. Box 40092
Cleveland, Ohio 44140
(216) 333-3155
© 1986, 1991, by Info-Tec., Inc.
ISBN 0-940017-14-8

Fourth Printing

PREFACE

With part-time and adjunct faculty assuming a greater and greater role in college teaching, educational institutions are assuming increased responsibility in providing support and assistance to this valuable human resource. The expertise and experience brought to the classroom by part-time faculty is of ever increasing importance to students and institutions. This expertise, however, can only adequately be appreciated if it is properly recognized and incorporated into the instructional process.

This document has been prepared specifically to assist adjunct faculty who have careers outside of education to understand efficiently many of the concepts necessary for effective teaching.

Realizing the time constraints facing part-time faculty, this booklet intentionally is brief but to-the-point. Instructors interested in examining the teaching process in greater detail may find the companion publication, *A Handbook for Adjunct and Part-Time Faculty and Teachers of Adults,* of value. It is the intent of the author that in some small way this publication assists faculty in realizing a successful and rewarding teaching experience.

—*Donald Greive, Ed.D.*

ABOUT THE AUTHOR

Donald Greive has spent the majority of his educational career as a faculty member and in administrative positions involving part-time faculty. He served as a Dean and Director of Evening and Continuing Education as well as Dean of Academic and Instructional Services. He has served as an adjunct faculty member at a liberal arts college, a state university, a community college and a technical institute. He has managed several national conferences on the topic of adjunct and part-time faculty.

He is the author of *A Handbook for Adjunct and Part-Time Faculty and Teachers of Adults*. Dr. Greive presently is a consultant for adjunct faculty development and management.

CONTENTS

CHARTS AND OUTLINES

INTRODUCTION

This document provides an efficient format for the enhancement and presentation of teaching strategies and techniques that have demonstrated effectiveness throughout the years. The booklet purposely is brief to allow part-time faculty a quick reference in readable format without extensive library research. In fact, many of the suggestions and hints have been proven in practice by successful teachers over the years but have little scientific or research documentation. Most of the topics discussed are covered in greater depth in *A Handbook for Adjunct and Part-Time Faculty and Teachers of Adults*.

Who am I??? . . . A part-time faculty member.
  If I'm early, no one notices. — If I'm late, everyone does.
  If I'm prepared for 101 — I'm assigned 102.
  If bowling or bridge is on Tuesday — my class is on Tuesday.
  If I have 25 handouts prepared — there are 26 in the class.
  If I am well prepared — the class is cancelled.
  If I am under-prepared — 53 people register.

But I am invaluable! In fact, in some institutions I am responsible for 50 percent of the total credit hours taught. I teach anytime, any section, any students. Often, I teach after a full day of employment or homemaking. Equally as often, I bring new skills, energy and expertise to the institution in which I am employed.

Why do I teach ??? . . . I want to share my expertise, ability and skills with other members of my culture; I want to help bridge the gap between the academic world and the community surrounding it; I want to share my talents with other citizens; I want to experience new frontiers . . . and most of all I love it!

FACULTY CHECKLIST

Listed below are several points that adjunct faculty may wish to review prior to commencing each teaching assignment. Familiarity with this information provides for a more effective and efficient teaching situation. Faculty may add additional items to their personal checklists as is deemed appropriate to individual teaching situations.

1. When are grades due? When do students receive grades?

2. Is there a college or departmental grading policy?

3. Is there a departmental course syllabus, course outline or statement of goals and objectives available for the course?

4. Are there prepared course handouts?

5. Are there prepared departmental tests?

6. What is the library book checkout procedure?

7. What instructional support aids are available?

8. What are the bookstore policies?

9. Is there a department and/or college attendance or tardiness policy?

10. Where are copies of the text and support materials obtained?

11. Where are instructional aid materials, films, video tapes, etc. obtained and what is the lead time for ordering?

12. What are the names of the department chairperson, dean, other college officials?

13. Is all of my paperwork for official employment completed (an expected paycheck that doesn't arrive is demoralizing).

STRATEGIES FOR TEACHING

Listed below are guidelines for classroom teachers which are presented to allow you to assess your own personality and teaching style in light of the realities of higher education. The guidelines are:

Your role as a teacher is that of a facilitator of learning. Knowing how to develop learning skills and teaching students to learn and organize their materials is more important than being the world's greatest expert in your field. To be a good facilitator of learning, read about the teaching profession. Read literature on learning; understand the varied student types.

Your teaching effectiveness is situational. Remember no two classes are alike. Adjust to your students early in the course, whether they are highly motivated to achieve professional advancement, or they are groping to establish themselves as college students. Determine if they need significant remedial and personal assistance.

Whether you like it or not, you are an actor or actress on stage. You have all of the responsibilities to and control of your audience as does a professional actor. Your appearance, your conduct, your communication techniques, use of your voice and your physical traits are constantly under scrutiny. Be aware that you are the star of the show.

Use humor delicately. In general, almost any joke will offend someone in your classroom. Humor may be used tactfully to relieve stressful situations; however, to depend upon jokes as entertainment to hold class attention is an indication of weakness.

Vary your teaching activities. This chapter later presents some suggestions for variation of classroom activities. Just changing the format of activities to get "out of a rut" is effective in maintaining student motivation and interest. Use the full line of audio visual support, e.g., films, video tapes, audio material, guest speakers, field trips. All of these resources enhance the learning situation.

Be sensitive to barriers. Many students bring obstacles to their learning. Some are visibly handicapped, and others are handicapped in less obvious ways. Be sensitive to these barriers, but do not be overly sympathetic. Some ways to be aware of barriers include:

   a. Be alert to early signs of poor progress in students and provide timely assistance.

   b. Be aware of the time management concerns of students. Be sure students understand time requirements, but don't frighten them away with unrealistic time demands.

   c. Be knowledgeable of college policies and procedures. Assist students concerning such activities as the library and dropping and adding classes.

   d. Try to recognize and assist students with limitations of learning abilities such as writing, reading and math. Students can be referred for appropriate help before it affects their class standing.

   e. Be aware that many students may be under significant stress. Avoid confrontations. Be considerate in dealing with such students.

   f. Handicapped students many times do not wish to disclose their handicap. Be sensitive to their needs. At the beginning of the class, it is a good technique to simply comment, "If anyone needs special seating, etc., see me after the class."

INTRODUCTION TO TEACHING

It is a commonly accepted axiom that learning is best accomplished when there is a need for learning and when it is built upon former learning and knowledge. Thus, it is evident that true learning is the responsiblity of students and not wholly that of the teacher. Teachers, however, are necessary for the learning process to take place. Whether one is a natural-born teacher who possesses the skills and techniques to walk in front of a group and perform, or whether one must work and over-prepare to reach the objectives are not important. In either case, in order to affect the learning process, certain professional skills and knowledge are necessary. Engineers or lawyers cannot walk into the middle of an engineering experiment or law case without special preparation; likewise, instructors cannot expect to succeed in teaching without an arsenal of knowledge concerning student learning and pedagogical skills.

The critical difference between the teaching profession and other professions, however, is quite simple. Most of our culturally accepted professions are heavily content oriented. With an adequate mastery of subject matter, theory, application and a considerable amount of devotion and hard work, one can succeed. In the world of teaching those factors are also necessary; however, they are useless without the additional ingredients of personality and the ability to communicate with other human beings. Thus, to be an effective teacher, it is necessary that one be multi-talented and multi-disciplined.

Essentially, the basic characteristics of good teaching are quite simple. They are:

- Knowing one's subject content
- Knowing and liking students

- Understanding one's culture
- Possessing command of professional teaching skills and strategies.

The First Class. It is normal that when one begins a teaching assignment and faces the first class there will be a considerable amount of anxiety and nervousness. Most teachers feel that this nervousness is a positive factor. In fact, many experienced teachers maintain that they do their best work when they start a class with a little anxiety.

Some basic guidelines that will assist an instructor to overcome anxiety and produce an effective and profitable meeting with the first class are to:

- Be over-prepared rather than under-prepared.
- Plan an activity that allows students to get involved immediately. This may simply be an information gathering session.
- Initiate casual conversation between you and students and among the students prior to launching into the specifics of the course.
- Develop an anecdote or an attempt at communication to bridge a common gap, such as a trip, a concert attended, a sports event, a current news event or a college happening.
- Acknowledge confusion at the beginning of class. Confusion is not detrimental. It is part of the "cooling in" process as students reduce anxieties with each other.
- Distribute syllabus.
- Conduct the class. Don't meet and dismiss. First impressions are most lasting.
- Present the goals and objectives of the course on

an overhead transparency and clarify with class discussion.

Instructors should not hesitate to share their background with the class. This eliminates the long process of students trying to "psych out" the professor. It also shows that the instructor is willing to share information as well as gather it. However, at no time should college teachers ask for more information from students about their professional and personal backgrounds than the instructors are willing to give about themselves.

Reducing anxieties sometimes involves what is called "setting the tone" of the classroom. Creative and positive feelings about the course and the expectations of the course are important. Professional appearance and a process for initiating activity is an additional positive factor. (*A personal note: It is important to communicate to the class that you are a friendly, helpful person and not hung-up as a disciplinarian, whether it be in the academic or behavioral sense. There are two extremes in teacher behavior that must be avoided. They are: The traditionally rigid "stay in your place" strategy and the laissez-faire "what shall we do today gang" approach. In teaching, the middle road is the only successful road.*)

Student characteristics. Teachers in today's colleges are dealing with few certainties. However, one of the certainties that exists is the fact that instructors will most likely face a diverse group of students. Students' backgrounds and aspirations are significantly different from those of the typical "college students" of a few years ago. One constantly must be concerned about the inadvertent tendency to stereotype students or classes. Such stereotyping can lead to problems in instruction and evaluation of students. Many students today are not sure of their own potential; thus, any tendency to stereotype is detrimental to both the students and the faculty member.

Listed below are four common characteristics that may be found in today's college students:

1. Today's college students probably will have a better grasp and concept of where they are going and why they are in class than in the past. They may be easily "put down" or become frustrated if their expectations are not met.

2. Today's college students view themselves much like consumers. They feel they have purchased a product and they will expect its delivery.

3. To some degree, they come to class more mature and more willing to share their rich life experiences. Many times these experiences and knowledge can be a valuable asset to the class.

4. College teachers must keep in mind that they are teaching adults not "kids." Very often adult students rebel at picky rules and standards that do not seem to contribute to the educational process.

CLASSROOM STRATEGIES

Overhead Projector. Overhead transparencies are valuable assets to classroom presentations. They are an efficient and effective method to convey information because they involve students in the visual as well as the audio learning mode. Instructors may utilize overhead transparencies when making a series of discussion points or when emphasizing important facts. Transparencies should be used as references for — or to highlight points in — classroom discussions, not simply to read lists of topics.

Overhead transparencies should be prepared to complement the overall lesson plan. Transparencies can be constructed simply by writing the contents on sheets of paper and reproducing them on a modern copier. Most learning resource centers have such capabilities. A professional touch can be added by typesetting those transparencies that will be used frequently. As a rule, a typewriter does not produce an effective overhead transparency.

The Laboratory. Effective laboratory instruction is the ultimate project activity that can be planned for any classroom situation. The first five letters of the word laboratory form the word LABOR, which is the key to successful lab instruction.

Instilling a serious attitude in students is a major goal of laboratory instruction. Regardless of the curriculum or the course being taught, some overall principles of laboratory instruction remain constant. They are:

1. The ability to explain clearly the directions and purposes of each session, including the objectives. This explanation might include written and verbal instructions and the development of a lab manual.

2. The ability to question and to interpret students' progress throughout the process of the laboratory activity.

3. The ability to present an effective demonstration emphasizing important points. This step also might include the assistance of a lab aide or technician.

4. The ability to sense when support is needed so student progress can continue.

5. The ability to make certain that appropriate tasks are developed for each student.

An effective method of maintaining student productivity is to award a grade to each student for each laboratory session. The grade is determined through observation by the instructor. It includes: an evaluation of the quality of work for the day, the quantity of work for the day, and the work attitude exhibited. A simple 1,2,3 can be awarded to each student for each lab session.

Partner System. Recently there has been an increased realization that students learn from each other as well as from their instructors. By working together, students' interests and achievements can be improved within the classroom. In addition to the small group techniques described later, some instructors find that assigning students to work in pairs, or partners, throughout the course greatly enhances students' progress. This technique can be implemented early in the course through voluntary mutual selection by the students, lottery, or other suitable methods. This system provides each student with a "partner" from whom to seek help and with whom to share ideas as he or she proceeds through the course.

Finally, some of the most effective classroom strategies are creative and self-developed by the instructors. Too often instruction consists mainly of imitating other instructors that one has had in his or her own collegiate learning experience. Such imitation limits the opportunity to try new and different teaching techniques. Many educators feel that activities in a classroom should change every 20 minutes. A teacher should not feel obligated to stay with traditional or time-proven classroom methods. (*If you feel like trying an innovative approach, share it with your students! They will be cooperative and appreciative of the fact that you are risk taking and innovative in your instructional endeavors.*)

STUDENT CLASSROOM BEHAVIORS

To be certain, teaching is a demanding activity. Most professionals can succeed in respective fields of endeavor with thorough knowledge of the technical and intellectual content of their professions. A teacher, however, requires this same competence, plus the ability to manage large numbers of individuals with divergent learning and behavior patterns. This section discusses some of the more common student behaviors in today's classrooms.

The Class Expert. The class expert is one who will have comment and knowledge concerning nearly any topic raised in class discussion. The instructor must be careful not to "put down" these students because it will discourage other students from contributing. Usually, an effective technique is to allow the "expert" to respond and allow peer pressure to eventually limit his/her activities. If this approach does not solve the problem, an individual conference after the second or third class session may be necessary. If all else fails, a verbal request in class for consideration of other students would be in order. Prepared objectives, to which everyone's attention must be addressed, are a vital asset.

The Quiet Class. Quiet classes are commonly encountered by part-time instructors due to the fact that many of the students returning are older and, as a result, insecure. Nonetheless, it is important that students verbalize as conversation and involvement is important to the learning process and provides feedback for the teacher.

As stated previously, the first class can be important in breaking the silence barrier before it starts. Some techniques to implement communication include: small group work, the partner system, discussions of current events and personal experiences, brainstorming, icebreakers, and instructor's anecdotes.

Negative Students. Negative student behavior manifests itself in diverse ways. Sometimes students will challenge class discussion in a negative manner, and, in other situations, they merely will remain silent and appear to sulk for no apparent reason. It is important that the instructor not allow the negative student syndrome to affect the class. The silent, negative student usually will not greatly affect the class; however, the negative verbal student will. Initially, efforts should be made to involve the negative student in a positive or success-oriented question/answer format. Through this technique, the instructor may be able to assess the interests of negative students and stimulate participation. (Remember, the negative student made the effort to register for the course and to attend the class; thus he or she brings positive attributes.) An individual conference with the student often can clarify and help resolve the matter.

The Unruly Student. Although it is not commonplace, an unruly student occasionally surfaces even in the college-level classroom. His or her behavior can manifest itself through disagreements with other students (possibly physical), verbal outbursts, cursing or general disruption. The instructor should exhaust all reasonable strategies to control the situation, such as: directing attention in silence, politely asking for cooperation, or private consultation. If conditions gravitate to the point at which classroom order no longer can be maintained, the instructor may ask the rest of the class to leave the room and then address the student with the problem in more direct ways in concert with procedures established by the institution.

CLASSROOM TECHNIQUES

The Lecture. The lecture is the most used and the most efficient of teaching techniques. One should not hesitate to use this technique even though it has the reputation of being overused. A good lecture requires more preparation than a good activity or demonstration. Some important points that must be kept in mind in preparing an effective lecture are:

1. Assess the background and experience of the students so that your lecture can be directed to their level.

2. Use anecdotes, concrete examples and dramatic contrast to emphasize points. Use gestures and eye contact to keep communication channels open with the class.

3. Use questions to stimulate and motivate students. Above all, summarize at the conclusion of every major part of the lecture. An effective summary includes repetition and reinforcement of the important points covered.

4. Be conscious of your vocabulary. This is especially important to faculty who are teaching in specialized areas where professional jargon and buzz words are in common use but may not be understood by students.

Question/answer. Proper use of questions is probably the most effective teaching mechanism in existence. Proper questioning is the ultimate of good communication. Several points to remember in questioning:

1. Use specific questions to individuals, not general questions to the class.

2. Use questions for all purposes: to arouse curiosity; to assess the class understanding of your

presentation; to evaluate the comprehension of students; to allow students to provide input and to expand upon the class contribution.

3. Use questions creatively whenever possible. A key question or an unusual question in each class session, even to the point of making a production of it, is effective in stimulating classes and conveying information.

4. Use open-ended questions to supplement lectures. These are questions that allow students to comment or respond to the opening rather than to give a short correct or incorrect answer. This type of question would be, "What do you think of that?" or "How does that strike you?" Then call upon your students by name.

Discussion Groups. Discussion techniques developed over the last twenty years have become a major part of good teaching. The most effective discussion is usually developed through the formation of small groups (three to six students) within the class. These discussions facilitate sharing and understanding, as well as application and reinforcement. Several points that should be remembered in developing a discussion format:

1. There must be an objective or purpose for the discussion; otherwise, it will deteriorate into meaningless buzz sessions and aimless sharing of opinions.

2. A case study is an excellent vehicle for the development of a meaningful discussion.

3. A controversial issue is effective as long as rational, logical conclusions are to be written at the end of the discussion.

4. It is a good idea to involve students in the development of the discussion format including

planning the activities, monitoring the discussion and presenting conclusions.

5. The evaluation plan of the course should be clearly developed so that students know exactly the value of the discussion in relation to their final grades.

PLANNING

Although there are few absolutes in the profession of teaching, one element of teaching receives universal agreement by experts and practioners: the importance of planning. If learning is to take place, adequate planning is necessary on the part of the college teacher to assure there is a process that leads to the desired learning outcomes. With today's sophisticated student clientele, teachers who depend upon "off the cuff teaching" are doomed to fail. *Although there are many planning support mechanisms, they are all essentially built upon one premise: to adequately plan the class process, one should first define the destination at which he or she desires to arrive and then develop a plan to reach that destination.* The three major parts of a formal teaching plan are the lesson plan, the course outline, and the course syllabus.

The lesson plan. The format for the lesson plan may vary depending upon the instructor and the type of course being taught. Several factors are universally agreed upon to comprise a good lesson plan: it should be written down; it should have a definite purpose, indicating the main thoughts for the lesson; and it should be numbered and arranged as part of the total plan for the course. The lesson plan may be formal or informal. For example, references, research and quotes may be part of the formal lesson plan. At the same time, anecdotal comments simply may be written in as marginal notes.

Outside references such as newspaper items may be clipped and handled as a unique entity.

The lesson plan allows the faculty member the greatest amount of freedom in the educational process. An effective lesson plan should reflect the creativity and the unique ideas of the faculty member. As was indicated earlier, just as one would not depend upon other faculty members' processes and techniques in teaching, one would not depend upon outside lesson plans. A good self-test for faculty who wish to determine their readiness for class is simply to ask themselves the same question often posed by students, "What are we going to do today — and why?" Essentially, a lesson plan should contain several parts. They are:

1. A list of definitions that should be clarified for the students.
2. The objectives of the class.
3. The activities in which each student will participate.
4. A definite plan for the activities of the instructor.
5. The impact or purpose of the class.
6. The assignment for the next session.

Following is a suggested lesson plan format that might be used by faculty members in preparation for classes.

SUGGESTED LESSON PLAN FORMAT

Course number and name
(after first page simply number chronologically)

_____

Date _____

Session # _____

Definitions to be covered _____

_____

Class objective(s) _____

_____

Student activities or exercises _____

_____

Instructor activities _____

_____

Major impact or thought _____

_____

Assignment _____

_____

The lesson plans for a course should be accumulated and kept chronologically in a permanent file or notebook. It is not necessary to develop completely new lesson plans each time the course is taught. However, by maintaining the lesson plans in chronological order, they are available for easy reference and for review and update as each new class is faced. Through this process, faculty will find that some of the material becomes outdated and, as new material is placed in the plan, a decision must be made concerning the elimination of less useful material.

The course outline. While the lesson plan is a daily map for teachers to ensure their direction and activity in a given session, the course outline is much more comprehensive and allows faculty to monitor the map of the entire course. Course outlines allow faculty, in a structured format, to add and include their personal, professional research as it is related to class topics.

Unlike the lesson plan, the course outline is very often a formal document that is developed at the departmental, division or program level. The outline normally is extracted from the course objectives. The general topical form usually is used with no greater detail than two or three subtopics.

Faculty must be concerned when developing a class outline whether their course is to be structured in a chronological or topical format. A chronological format requires that learning is built upon prior related information, whereas a topical outline can be modified and rearranged with much more flexibility (related to topics and tasks) without undue concern about ordering or time sequence.

Following is an example of a course outline developed in sufficient detail for most applications.

SAMPLE COURSE OUTLINE

Statistics

I. Introduction
   A. Basic statistics
      1. Purposes
   B. Data gathering
      1. Samples
      2. Recorded data
II. Presenting data
   A. Tables
      1. Summary tables
         a. Table elements
         b. Tables with averages
   B. Graphs
      1. Types of graphs
         a. Bar
         b. Pie chart
         c. Line
      2. Data presentation with graphs
   C. Frequency distribution
      1. Discrete and continuous
      2. Class interval

The course syllabus. A syllabus is defined as "a concise statement of the main points of a course of study or subject." The syllabus is the official document for the course; whereas, the lesson plan is an instrument of the instructor for day-to-day operation. The course outline is a specific guideline for the course content. The syllabus to some degree is a combination of the two. The syllabus should be shared with students and should be a permanent part of the instructional archives of the campus. In fact, it may even become a legal document in the event litigation arises as a result of consumer (student) complaints.

Although the syllabus is the most important document in the instructional process, it has varied styles and formats depending upon the institution and/or individual preparing it. Despite the varied styles, however, there is agreement that a syllabus should contain several main parts. They are:

1. The complete name of the course, including the course number.
2. The name and title by which the faculty member wishes to be addressed.
3. The faculty member's office hours.
4. The text or texts and manuals required.
5. The course requirements and grading standards.
6. The course objectives.
7. The specific assignments, projects, etc., to be completed by students.
8. A complete listing of resources, outside readings, field trips, etc.

A partial example of a syllabus follows:

ACHIEVEMENT UNIVERSITY
Syllabus

Name of Course:
    History 200

Faculty Name:
    Dr. Madeline Jones — Dr. Jones

Office Hours:
    MWF 8:00-9:00 a.m., 2:00-3:00 p.m.
    TR 1:00-2:00 p.m.

Text:
    (Author, name, edition, publisher)

Course Requirements:
    Outside readings (general and reserved lists, projects)

Grading:
    Midterm — essay, 30% of final grade
    Final — multiple choice, 30% of final grade
    Class project and class participation (including quizzes) — 40% of final grade

Course objectives: (to be inserted)

Student Exercises:
    Completion of all examinations, quizzes and projects listed under requirements. The completion of the reading of texts, specific assignments by class session listed, and outside readings as assigned. Submission of an eight-page topic paper (insert date) selected from a list of topics distributed in the class.

Resource readings:
    (Listing of text, outside readings, reserved materials, special reference materials and personal resources outside of the classroom).

The syllabus should be distributed to the students the first day of class. Time should be taken to discuss the syllabus and details therein. In fact, it is also a good practice to go over the syllabus the second meeting of the class. It is necessary to describe in detail the activities of the students as they relate to certain assignments and objectives. A syllabus is a scientific document and a work of art, and it should be shown that respect in its development and use.

Faculty self-evaluation. Any process that is dynamic, whether it be in teaching or elsewhere, is of little value unless the process can be evaluated to determine success. The planning process in teaching is no exception. If one is to adequately plan, expending hours of time, energy and research, it is only appropriate that faculty receive some indication of the fruits of that planning. One of the methods to evaluate the planning process is self-evaluation.

Although many colleges have faculty evaluation forms that they either require or recommend for use, faculty, in terms of assessing their own planning, may wish to develop a self-evaluation form. When administering the form, the students should be informed that this is a teaching-evaluation exercise; thus, only constructive criticism or reinforcement is of value to the instructor. Even though student opinions are very often biased, there is no question of the value of student input. Most students will respond honestly and sincerely and, like any other statistical technique, over the period of several courses the deviant responses can be identified.

A suggested faculty evaluation form is included here. It is not intended that these are the only questions to be asked or that statistical validity has been tested. It is, however, suggested that faculty develop an instrument for their own use. A few underlying principles should be observed. They are:

1. The form should not be so long that students eventually check anything to complete the form.

2. It should be logically organized into classroom, course related, and personal evaluation.

3. The evaluation code should be simple and easily understood. Excessive numbering such as 1-10 is only confusing. A simple 1-5 is easily understood by the students.

4. It should, of course, be anonymous and should be given prior to the class session during which the final examination is held.

FACULTY SELF-EVALUATION FORM

CLASS: _____ DATE: _____

INSTRUCTIONS: Please grade each factor on a scale of 1-5 (5 being highest) in terms of your perception of the teacher's behavior or characteristics.

CLASSROOM EVALUATION
Preparation for class   _____
Communication of classroom expectations   _____
Command of subject matter   _____
Professional and businesslike classroom behavior _____
Tests and evaluations reflect classroom lectures,
discussions and objectives   _____
Availability for consultation   _____
Encouragement of student participation   _____
Assignments clear and concise   _____

COURSE-RELATED FACTORS
Appropriateness of project assignments   _____
Value of field trips   _____
Appropriate topic selection for outside
assignments   _____
Utilization of supplemental teaching aids,
support and other activities   _____

TEACHER EVALUATION
Consideration for differing opinions   _____
Consideration for individuals as persons   _____
Sense of humor   _____
Rating of instructor as compared to other
college professors   _____
Personal appearance   _____
Instructor's greatest strengths _____
_____
Instructor's greatest weaknesses _____
_____
Suggestions to improve course _____
_____

REFERENCES

Greive, Donald. *A Handbook for Adjunct and Part-Time Faculty and Teachers of Adults.* Cleveland: Box 40092, Info-Tec, Inc., 1990.

OTHER EDUCATIONAL PRODUCTS
FROM
INFO-TEC

☐ A Handbook For Adjunct/Part-Time Faculty
and Teachers of Adults. (Rev. 1990)

☐ Teaching in College -
A Resource for College Teachers. (Rev. 1989)

☐ The Magic Gradebook
(Micro-Computer Grading).

☐ Cultural Diversity Manual.

☐ Total Quality Education -
Teaching Techniques for Technical Educators.

☐ Cooperative Learning
A Classroom Guide.